great balls of cheese

great balls of cheese

michelle buffardi

photography by jason wyche

HOUGHTON MIFFLIN HARCOURT
Boston • New York

This book is printed on acid-free paper.

Copyright © 2013 by Michelle Buffardi.

Photography copyright © 2013 by Jason Wyche

Food styling by Joyce Sangirardi

Prop styling by Kira Corbin

Interior design and layout by Kara Plikaitis

Published by Houghton Mifflin Harcourt Publishing Company

Published simultaneously in Canada

www.hmhco.com

For information about permission to reproduce selections from this book, write to Permissions, Houghton Mifflin Harcourt Publishing Company, 215 Park Avenue South, New York, New York 10003.

Library of Congress Cataloging-in-Publication Data:

Buffardi, Michelle, 1979–

  Great balls of cheese / Michelle Buffardi.

     pages cm

  Includes index.

  ISBN 978-1-118-49720-3 (hbk.); ISBN 978-0-544-18666-8 (ebk.)

  1. Cheese. I. Title.

  TX759.5.C48B84 2013

  641.3'73--dc23

                                    2012045308

Printed in China

TOP 10 9 8 7 6 5 4

4500771316

dedication

For Deb—
Thank you for always being supportive
of my cheesiness.

acknowledgments

Once I got started thinking about cheese balls, I wasn't able to stop. If you thumb through this book, you'll see what the inside of my head looks like, or at least has looked like for the past two years. I dream in cheese. I think in terms of cheese. And when I see an object, such as a cat or Christmas ornament, or a stranger on the train with a particularly round head, I imagine it as cheese.

For a girl who dreams in cheese, this book is a dream come true, and I owe many people a debt of gratitude for making it happen.

Deb, for making this possible, and for always pushing me, nicely, in the ways I need to be pushed. Thank you for being a mentor and friend. To all of my coworkers for their support, inspiration, and cheese ball enthusiasm, and especially to Bob and Sharon for having my back.

Justin Schwartz, my patient, smart, cheese-loving editor and early-on believer, and Stacy Glick, my agent, who both understood me immediately and guided me through the process of writing a cookbook so well that it almost seemed easy (it wasn't).

Jason Wyche, who managed to photograph cheese to be both beautiful and funny. Kira Corbin, a brilliant prop stylist who took the time to get to know me (and taught me that I like the color blue). Joyce Sangirardi, who styled every single one of the cheese balls on these pages just as I wanted them—some even better—and her super-patient assistant Marianne Zanzarella, who mixed, by hand, dozens of cheese balls, which was no easy task.

Gregory, my best friend and coconspirator, who has let me boss him around in the kitchen for almost half of our lives, and who went above and beyond to help me create the recipes in this book.

My parents—all four of them—who inspired and supported a somewhat appropriate balance of creative and crazy. Thank you for always believing in me. To the rest of my family and friends: You're welcome for the months of cheesy snacks, and thank you for being great.

And to Bob Powers, whose love makes my life better.

introduction

ACCORDING TO LEGEND, the first cheese ball in recorded history was made in 1801 by Elisha Brown Jr. on his farm and presented to President Thomas Jefferson. This alleged cheese ball weighed 1,235 pounds. The next cheese ball served after this (unverified) historical moment was likely made by someone's grandma for a holiday gathering. It was probably covered in nuts and clocked in at around 1½ pounds.

Somewhere along the way, "cheese ball" became associated with the "uncool"—a term reserved for bad jokes, ugly gifts that beg to be regifted, or hideous patterns on a tablecloth or skirt. But the appetizer that is literally a ball of cheese deserves much more respect. Cheese is as fashionable as ever, and a make-ahead appetizer that requires little prep and, in most cases, no cooking and no special equipment or skill, and that makes us think fondly on the holiday gatherings of our youth deserves its chance in the spotlight.

cheese ball basics

An idea as simple as a ball of cheese shouldn't be overthought, but there are some key rules to keep in mind.

THE CHEESE BALL: Cheese balls can be savory or sweet, and the term "balls" is used loosely—cheese can be molded into various shapes, like animals, trees, snowmen, or logs, in varying sizes. The large cheese balls in this book can all be made into "minis" for a bite-sized presentation, or logs if you prefer.

THE METHOD: You can use a stand mixer, a handheld mixer, or a spatula and a bowl to mix your cheese ball. I don't recommend using a food processor to blend your ingredients; it will work, but it whizzes the cheeses up too much and the mixture will take much longer to set up. Refrigerating your cheese balls before serving is a must—the softened cream cheese needs to be chilled for the best texture, the mix-ins need a chance to mingle together for the best flavor, and a firm cheese ball will hold its shape the best. Cheese balls don't take long to make, but if you're planning on serving one, think ahead: At least two hours chilling time in the fridge is ideal.

THE CHEESE: The base for most cheese balls is a soft cheese, usually cream cheese, because it's malleable, mild flavored, and firms up nicely in the fridge. In all the recipes that follow, I call for regular cream cheese, but if you want a lighter, less-rich cheese ball, you can substitute low-fat or Neufchâtel cheese; I don't recommend fat-free cream cheese because the results will be a bit grainy and won't taste as great. Soft cheeses, like cream cheese or goat cheese, should be softened before you make your cheese ball; it will be much easier to mix that way. Leave your soft cheese on the counter for an hour or so; hard cheeses (like cheddar) don't need to be left out.

Cream cheese can stand alone, but in many recipes another cheese or combination of cheeses is used. Cheddar, Swiss, Manchego, blue, and goat cheeses are used as both stabilizers to help the ball hold its shape and to add flavor. Don't feel like you have to go to a specialty cheese shop to shop for a cheddar cheese that you're going to mold into an owl; the cheese sold at the grocery store will suffice. But I will hold firm that you should buy your cheese in brick form and shred it yourself; the preshredded kind has additives to keep it from sticking together in the package, and that affects the flavor and texture of your cheese ball. Take the extra few minutes to shred the cheese yourself.

THE COATING: Most cheese balls are coated in something—nuts, seeds, chopped herbs, or crushed cookies or crackers—for flavor and texture. Don't coat your cheese ball, or decorate it for that matter, until you're ready to serve it or the coating (or decorations) will get mushy. If you're bringing a cheese ball to a party, keep the ball and the coating in separate containers and assemble just before serving. And a word or two on nuts: Always toast your nuts. This goes for cheese balls and most other things. Toasted nuts have a deeper, nuttier (yes, nuttier) flavor, so don't skip this step.

cheese balls

the appetizer that is
literally a ball of cheese deserves
much more respect

savory recipes

eight-ball cheese ball

If you want a black-as-night coating on your eight-ball you can use black sesame seeds here, but they're pretty expensive, so I use poppy seeds, which also happen to work really well with the cream cheese–think cream cheese on a poppy seed bagel.

serves
15 to 20

- 16 ounces cream cheese, softened

- 1 cup shredded mozzarella cheese

- 2 garlic cloves, minced or pressed through a garlic press

- Pinch coarse salt

- ¼ cup poppy seeds, for coating

- 1 colossal black olive, pitted, for decorating

Crackers, for serving

Using a stand mixer or a bowl and a spatula, mix together the cream cheese, mozzarella, garlic, and salt until smooth. Form the mixture into a ball, cover with plastic wrap, and chill for at least 2 hours or overnight.

To decorate: Cut a 3-inch circle out of wax paper and press into the top of the cheese ball. Pour the poppy seeds into a bowl, add the cheese ball, and swirl the bowl gently to coat the cheese ball. The poppy seeds should cover the entire ball; the wax paper will protect the circle so it stays white. Once the ball is coated, put it on a serving plate and gently remove the wax paper. Slice 2 thin slices, widthwise, from the olive, and arrange them in the white circle to look like the number "8."

Serve with crackers.

mexican black bean ball

Also called "Everything That's Great about a Burrito in Cheese Ball Form."

Using a stand mixer or a bowl and a spatula, mix together the cheddar, beans, cream cheese, onion, 2 tablespoons cilantro (reserve the rest for coating the cheese ball), cumin, salt, and cayenne, if using, until combined. Form the mixture into a ball, cover with plastic wrap, and refrigerate for at least 2 hours or overnight.

Before serving, coat the cheese ball in the remaining cilantro.

Serve with crackers or pita chips.

- 2 cups shredded extra-sharp cheddar cheese

- One 15-ounce can black beans, drained and rinsed

- 8 ounces cream cheese, softened

- 2 tablespoons minced red onion

- ¾ cup chopped fresh cilantro

- 2 teaspoons ground cumin

- ¼ teaspoon coarse salt

- Pinch cayenne pepper (optional)

Crackers or pita chips, for serving

buffalo chicken cheese ball

Buffalo chicken anything is amazing—Buffalo chicken macaroni and cheese, Buffalo chicken pizza, Buffalo chicken salad, Buffalo chicken sandwiches—so naturally, a great big ball of Buffalo chicken and cheese joins the ranks of foods made better with wing sauce.

serves
15 to 20

- 2 cups finely shredded cooked chicken

- ¾ cup buffalo wing sauce, such as Frank's RedHot Wings sauce

- 12 ounces cream cheese, softened

- 2 cups shredded sharp cheddar cheese

- 3 ounces blue cheese

- 1 bunch scallions, chopped, 1 tablespoon of the white part of the scallions reserved

Celery sticks, carrot sticks, and crackers, for serving

Toss the chicken in the wing sauce until coated. Using a stand mixer or a bowl and a spatula, blend the chicken mixture, cream cheese, cheddar, blue cheese, and the 1 tablespoon of the reserved white parts of the chopped scallions. Form the mixture into a ball, cover with plastic wrap, and refrigerate for at least 2 hours or overnight.

Before serving, roll the cheese ball in the remaining scallions.

Serve with celery and carrot sticks and crackers. This cheese ball is quite hearty, so you'll need a knife for serving.

herbed caterpillar

Fresh herbs are key here—the bright green color not only looks really nice, but the herbs also brighten the flavor of the feta and lemon. Don't worry too much about which herbs you use; choose a mixture of whatever green herbs you can find, or use all parsley—you can always find fresh parsley.

serves
15 to 20

- 16 ounces cream cheese, softened

- 2 cups chopped mixed fresh green herbs, such as dill, mint, and/or parsley

- 4 ounces feta cheese

- 1 garlic clove, minced

- 1 teaspoon fresh lemon juice

- Coarse salt and freshly ground black pepper, to taste

- 2 pretzel sticks, 1 dark raisin, and 1 small piece red bell pepper, for decorating

  Crackers or crudités, for serving

Using a stand mixer or a bowl and a spatula, blend the cream cheese, 2 tablespoons of the herbs, the feta, garlic, lemon juice, and salt and black pepper to taste. Form the mixture into 8 balls in descending sizes. Cover with plastic wrap and refrigerate for at least 2 hours or overnight.

Before serving, roll the balls in the remaining chopped herbs, leaving 1 medium-sized ball plain; this will be the head. Arrange the balls in descending order and place the plain ball on top of the largest for the head. Decorate the caterpillar face with the 2 pretzel sticks for the antennae, half of the raisin for each eye, and the tiny piece of red pepper for the nose.

Serve with crackers and crudités, such as carrots and broccoli.

chilly penguin

serves
15 to 20

If you prefer a sportier penguin, set this guy on two slices of red bell pepper to make him look like he's skiing, but if you want your penguin to chill, set him on feet made from sliced carrots.

Using a stand mixer or a bowl and a spatula, mix together the cream cheese, blue cheese, shallots, salt, and hot sauce. Form the mixture into a ball and cover with plastic wrap; refrigerate for at least 2 hours or overnight.

Before serving, remove a 2-inch piece of the cheese mixture, roll into a ball, and set aside; this will be the penguin's head. Re-form the remaining cheese mixture into an egg shape. Cut out a triangle shape roughly the length of your cheese ball from a sheet of wax paper. Press the wax paper into the cheese ball, with the widest part of the paper on the widest part of the cheese ball. Roll the cheese ball in the poppy seeds and set the ball on a plate. Slowly remove the wax paper; the ball should be covered in poppy seeds except for the penguin's breast. Set the head on top of the penguin's body and add the raisins for the eyes and the almond for the beak. Slice off 2 equal-sized rounds of the carrot and arrange them on either side of the head as earmuffs. Connect the earmuffs with the green part of the scallion. Using a vegetable peeler, peel 1 long strip off the carrot; wind this around the penguin's neck as a scarf. Slice the remaining carrot into toes and arrange at the bottom of the penguin's body to make its feet, or use two red bell pepper slices.

Serve with crackers.

- 16 ounces cream cheese, softened
- 4 ounces blue cheese
- 2 teaspoons chopped shallots
- ¼ teaspoon coarse salt
- Dash hot sauce, such as Frank's RedHot
- ½ cup poppy seeds, for coating
- 2 dark raisins, 1 almond, 1 carrot, 1 red bell pepper (optional), and 1 scallion, for decorating

Crackers, for serving

o christmas tree

Browse the produce aisle and you'll find that there's a bunch of jewel-toned fruits and vegetables fit for decorating a Christmas tree. I like to use multicolored bell peppers or pomegranate seeds, but you can use whatever inspires you. Star fruit, of course, is the natural choice for a tree topper.

serves
12 to 15

- 16 ounces cream cheese, softened

- 2 tablespoons chopped mixed fresh herbs, such as dill, oregano, and/or thyme

- 2 garlic cloves, minced

- 1 teaspoon Dijon mustard

- ½ teaspoon coarse salt

- 1 bunch fresh parsley, chopped, for coating

- Red, orange, or yellow bell pepper bits, 1 slice star fruit, and pomegranate seeds, for decorating

Crackers and crudités, for serving

Using a stand mixer or a bowl and a spatula, mix together the cream cheese, herbs, garlic, mustard, and salt until combined. Form the mixture into a ball, cover with plastic wrap, and refrigerate for at least 2 hours or overnight.

Before serving, form the ball into a tree shape—like an egg shape, but pointier on top. Roll the tree-shaped ball in the parsley, reshaping it with your hands as necessary. Decorate with bits of bell peppers and pomegranate seeds. Top with the slice of star fruit.

Serve with crackers and crudités.

cranberry & rosemary christmas ornament

serves
12 to 15

If Christmas had a flavor, I think it would be something like this combination of cranberry, goat cheese, and rosemary.

Using a stand mixer or a bowl and a spatula, mix together the cream cheese, goat cheese, cranberries, rosemary, and garlic until combined. Form the mixture into a ball and cover with plastic wrap. Refrigerate for at least 2 hours or overnight.

Before serving, decorate the cheese ball with small pieces of bell pepper and/or radishes. Fold the chive into a loop and stick it into the top of the ornament, forming a "hook."

Serve with crackers or baguette slices.

tip You can buy tiny cookie cutters in most kitchen supply stores or craft stores; they work well for cutting the peppers into shapes for decorating this and the Ham and Cheese Easter Egg cheese ball on page 42.

- 8 ounces cream cheese, softened
- 8 ounces goat cheese, softened
- ½ cup coarsely chopped dried cranberries
- ¼ teaspoon chopped fresh rosemary
- 1 small garlic clove, minced
- Small pieces multicolored bell peppers and/or radishes and 1 fresh chive, for decorating

Crackers or baguette slices, for serving

curried cheese ball

Some people think they don't like curry powder; they assume it's spicy—but it's *spiced*, not spicy. If you have those kinds of guests at a party, just call this a cheese ball and don't mention the curry until after they've eaten a whole bunch and want to know the source of the unbelievable flavor.

serves
15 to 20

- 16 ounces cream cheese, softened

- 1 cup shredded sharp cheddar cheese

- $\frac{1}{4}$ cup chopped dates

- 1 tablespoon finely chopped sweet onion

- 1 tablespoon mango chutney (optional)

- 1 $\frac{1}{2}$ teaspoons mild curry powder

- Pinch coarse salt

- Pinch cayenne pepper (optional)

- 1 cup chopped unsalted pistachios, toasted (see page 94), for coating

Crackers or crudités, for serving

Using a stand mixer or a bowl and a spatula, mix together the cream cheese, cheddar, dates, onion, mango chutney, if using, curry powder, salt, and cayenne, if using, until combined. Form the mixture into a ball and cover with plastic wrap. Refrigerate for at least 2 hours or overnight.

Before serving, roll the cheese ball in the pistachios to coat.

Serve with crackers or crudités.

goat cheese & blueberry log with balsamic-blueberry sauce

Dressing up a cheese ball with a sauce might seem as silly as putting your cat in a party dress, and I don't call for any other fancy accoutrements elsewhere in this book, but this blueberry sauce only takes a few minutes and is worth the trouble.

FOR THE CHEESE LOG:

- 8 ounces cream cheese, softened

- 6 ounces goat cheese, softened

- 1 cup fresh blueberries

- 1 teaspoon sugar

- ¼ teaspoon coarse salt

- 1 cup chopped pecans, toasted (see page 94), for coating

FOR THE BALSAMIC-BLUEBERRY SAUCE:

- 1 cup sugar

- ½ cup balsamic vinegar

- ½ cup fresh blueberries

Crackers or baguette slices, for serving

Using a stand mixer or a bowl and a spatula, mix together the cream cheese, goat cheese, blueberries, sugar, and salt. Form the mixture into a log, cover with plastic wrap, and refrigerate for at least 2 hours or overnight.

While the log is chilling, make the balsamic-blueberry sauce: Simmer the sugar, vinegar, and blueberries over low heat until the mixture reduces by half, about 30 minutes. Remove from the heat and let cool.

Before serving, roll the cheese log in the pecans and drizzle with the balsamic-blueberry sauce.

Serve with crackers or baguette slices.

greek bites

I love surprises—I think everyone does. The cheese part of these bites is savory and delicious on its own but then surprise! There's an olive inside.

Using a stand mixer or a bowl and a spatula, combine the cream cheese, feta, oregano, lemon zest, and wine, if using. Refrigerate the mixture for 1 hour.

Cut the olives in half. Using your fingers, wrap about 1 tablespoon of the cheese mixture around each olive half to cover. Refrigerate for 1 hour.

Before serving, roll each ball in the pine nuts. Spear each with a pretzel stick, if using, or toothpick and garnish with a mint leaf, if desired.

- 8 ounces cream cheese, softened
- 8 ounces feta cheese
- 1 tablespoon chopped fresh oregano
- Zest of 1 lemon, grated
- 1 tablespoon dry white wine (optional)
- 16 Kalamata olives, pitted
- 1 cup pine nuts, toasted (see page 94), for coating
- 32 thin pretzel sticks, for serving (optional)
- Fresh mint leaves, for decorating (optional)

ham & cheese easter egg

Decorating a giant Easter egg made of cheese is about a million times more fun than decorating regular old Easter eggs—plus the whole thing's edible.

Using a stand mixer or a bowl and a spatula, mix together the cream cheese, cheddar, minced ham, onion, mustard, and salt. Form the mixture into an egg shape, cover with plastic wrap, and refrigerate for at least 2 hours or overnight.

Before serving, decorate the cheese ball with bits of bell pepper, scallions, chives, and ham.

Serve with crackers.

- 16 ounces cream cheese, softened
- 1½ cups shredded sharp white cheddar cheese
- ¼ cup finely minced deli ham
- 1 tablespoon finely chopped onion
- 1 tablespoon Dijon mustard
- ¼ teaspoon coarse salt
- Peppers and chopped scallions, fresh chives, and 1 slice deli ham, for decorating

Crackers, for serving

tricolored pesto & sun-dried tomato terrine

special
equipment:
1 mini
loaf pan

serves
12 to 15

You can arrange the layers in whichever order you choose, but I like green, white, and red like the Italian flag, which seems fitting for these flavors.

FOR THE (GREEN) PESTO LAYER:

- 4 ounces cream cheese, softened
- ½ cup pesto (see page 83)

FOR THE (WHITE) GARLIC LAYER:

- 4 ounces cream cheese, softened
- 1 garlic clove, crushed

FOR THE (RED) SUN-DRIED TOMATO LAYER:

- ½ cup sun-dried tomatoes (not in oil)
- 1 garlic clove
- 1 teaspoon extra-virgin olive oil
- ½ teaspoon balsamic vinegar
- ½ teaspoon light brown sugar
- ½ teaspoon coarse salt
- 4 ounces cream cheese, softened

Pine nuts, for decorating

Baguette slices, for serving

Line a mini loaf pan with plastic wrap, leaving an overhang on all sides.

MAKE THE GREEN LAYER: Using a stand mixer or a bowl and a spatula, mix the cream cheese and pesto together until combined. Press the mixture into the bottom of the loaf pan; be careful not to smear the mixture on the sides of the pan. Refrigerate for 30 minutes.

MAKE THE WHITE LAYER: Mix the cream cheese and garlic together. Press the mixture into the pan, on top of the firm green layer, taking care not to smear the mixture on the sides of the pan. Refrigerate for 30 minutes.

MAKE THE RED LAYER: Using a food processor, combine the sun-dried tomatoes, garlic, oil, vinegar, sugar, and salt. Add the cream cheese and blend until combined. Press the tomato mixture into the loaf pan on top of the firm white layer, smooth the top, and refrigerate for at least 1 hour.

Before serving, overturn the loaf pan onto a platter and remove the plastic wrap. Garnish with the basil leaves and pine nuts, if desired.

Serve with baguette slices.

lox bagel ball

serves
12 to 15

A cheese ball made from the best bagel toppings makes for a much better presentation at brunch than a plain tub of cream cheese and piles of lox, onions, and capers. Beyond brunch, serve this with bagel chips or pita chips.

Using a stand mixer or a bowl and a spatula, mix together the cream cheese, salmon, onion, and capers. Form the mixture into a ball, cover with plastic wrap, and refrigerate for at least 2 hours or overnight.

Before serving, roll the cheese ball in the scallions to coat.

Serve with bagels, bagel chips, or pita chips.

- 16 ounces cream cheese, softened
- 4 ounces smoked salmon, chopped
- 2 tablespoons finely chopped red onion
- 2 tablespoons small capers, drained
- 1 bunch scallions, chopped, for coating

Bagels, bagel chips, or pita chips, for serving

spinach-artichoke ball

Everyone's favorite hot dip becomes everyone's favorite cheese ball.

serves
12 to 15

- One 10-ounce box frozen chopped spinach, thawed

- 16 ounces cream cheese, softened

- One 14-ounce can artichoke hearts (packed in water), drained and chopped

- ½ cup freshly grated Parmesan cheese

- 1 garlic clove, chopped

- 1 teaspoon fresh lemon juice

- ¼ teaspoon coarse salt

- Dash hot sauce, such as Frank's RedHot

- 8 to 10 tortilla chips, crushed, for coating

Pita chips or crackers, for serving

Place the spinach in a clean kitchen towel or sturdy paper towels and gather at the top. Squeeze the spinach to remove as much moisture as possible.

Using a stand mixer or a bowl and a spatula, mix together the spinach, cream cheese, artichoke hearts, Parmesan, garlic, lemon juice, salt, and hot sauce until combined. Form the mixture into a ball and wrap in plastic wrap; refrigerate for at least 2 hours or overnight.

Before serving, roll the cheese ball in the tortilla chips to coat.

Serve with pita chips or crackers. (Tortilla chips will break if you use them to scoop the cheese ball, but they'll hold if you spread the cheese onto the chip.)

tip FOR CRUSHING CHIPS, CRACKERS, OR COOKIES: Place chips (or crackers or cookies) in a resealable plastic bag, sealed nearly shut (you want to leave a tiny air hole so the bag doesn't pop). Roll over the chips in the bag with a rolling pin or a can until crushed.

mouse bites

Mice are associated with Swiss cheese for reasons I don't understand, but I do understand that Swiss cheese and Dijon mustard is a winning combination best served shaped like tiny mice with big sliced-almond ears and outlandishly long tails made from chives.

makes about 16 mice

- **8 ounces cream cheese, softened**
- **2 cups shredded Swiss cheese**
- **1 tablespoon chopped shallots**
- **1½ teaspoons Dijon mustard**
- **¼ teaspoons Worcestershire sauce**
- **¼ teaspoon coarse salt**
- **Crackers, for serving**
- **Black olive pieces, sliced almonds, and fresh chives, for decorating**

Using a stand mixer or a bowl and a spatula, mix together the cream cheese, Swiss, shallots, mustard, Worcestershire sauce, and salt until combined. Using a teaspoon, scoop out about sixteen 1-ounce balls of the cheese mixture and form into mouse shapes—teardrop-shaped balls of cheese about the size of your thumb. Place the mouse-shaped cheese balls on a baking sheet, cover with plastic wrap, and refrigerate for at least 2 hours or overnight.

Before serving, set each "mouse" on a cracker and decorate with a tiny piece of olive each for the eyes and nose, 2 sliced almonds for the ears, and a chive for the tail.

nacho cat

As far as pets go, I'm more of a dog person, but I'll take a cat in cheese ball form any time. The nacho-cheesy flavor of this cat works really well with tortilla chips, but if you try to dip a chip into this feline, it'll break. Instead, spread the cheese onto tortilla chips, or serve it with crackers instead.

Using a stand mixer or a bowl and a spatula, mix together the cream cheese, cheddar, onion, jalapeño, salsa, cumin, and salt until combined. Form the mixture into a ball, cover with plastic wrap, and refrigerate for at least 2 hours or overnight.

While the mixture is chilling, peel strips from the carrot to use as "stripes" on the cat and set aside. Peel the carrot until you reach the middle. Remove any bits of carrot sticking to the core of the carrot and reserve for the cat's tail.

Before serving, unwrap the cheese ball and break off a 3-ounce portion (about the size of a golf ball), roll into a ball, and set aside; this will be the cat's head. Form the remaining cheese mixture into an egg shape, and place on a plate. Arrange the reserved carrot strips on the egg shape to make the stripes. Attach the reserved carrot to the back of the cat for the tail. Place the reserved golf ball–sized cheese ball on top of the cat to make the head. Stick the chips in for the cat's ears. Cut the olive into eyes and a mouth and arrange on the cat's face. Finish with pieces of chives for the cat's whiskers.

Serve with crackers.

- 16 ounces cream cheese, softened
- 1½ cups shredded sharp cheddar cheese, preferably orange
- 1 tablespoon minced onion
- 1 jalapeño, cored, seeded, and chopped
- 1 tablespoon tomato salsa
- 2 teaspoons ground cumin
- Pinch coarse salt
- 1 carrot, 2 nacho cheese tortilla chips, 1 pitted black olive, and fresh chives, for decorating

Tortilla chips or crackers, for serving

wise (& cheesy) owl

Owls are nocturnal animals, meaning they come out only at night. The same rules do not apply to owl-shaped cheese balls; this guy makes a fitting afternoon party snack.

- 16 ounces cream cheese, softened

- 1 cup shredded extra-sharp cheddar cheese

- 2 tablespoons minced shallots

- 1 teaspoon Dijon mustard

- ½ teaspoon coarse salt

- ¼ teaspoon Worcestershire sauce

FOR DECORATING THE OWL:

- 1 cup sliced almonds, toasted (see page 94)

- 2 small round butter crackers, such as Ritz Bits

- 2 small pitted black olives, sliced

- 1 carrot

- 2 scoop-shaped corn chips, such as Fritos Scoops!

Crackers, for serving

Using a stand mixer or a bowl and a spatula, mix together the cream cheese, cheddar, shallots, mustard, salt, and Worcestershire sauce in a bowl. Set aside 1 teaspoon of the cream cheese mixture; you'll need this for the eyes. Form the remaining mixture into an owl shape—it should look like a large egg. Cover with plastic wrap and refrigerate for at least 2 hours or overnight.

When ready to serve, layer the almonds around the back and sides of the owl for the feathers, leaving the breast area plain. To make the eyes, spread each small butter cracker with half of the reserved cream cheese mixture, and stick an olive slice in the middle. Affix the eyes to where the owl's face will be. To make the beak, slice two ¼-inch pieces of the carrot into triangles, and make a mouth below the owl's eyes. To make the feet, slice 6 slivers from the remaining carrot and arrange at the bottom of the owl. Finish the owl by pressing the 2 corn chips into the head for ears.

Serve with crackers.

pimiento cheese chick

serves 12 to 15

Pimiento cheese is a staple in the South; it's usually made with cheddar cheese and mayonnaise (in addition to pimientos, of course) and spread on white bread. Add mayonnaise to a cheese ball and it won't hold its shape, so I've used cream cheese instead, and formed it into a chubby chick with shredded cheddar cheese "feathers" and an almond "beak."

Using a stand mixer or a bowl and a spatula, mix together 2 cups of the cheddar (reserve ½ cup for coating the cheese ball), the cream cheese, pimientos, onion, paprika, salt, and cayenne until combined. Remove a 2-inch piece of the cheese mixture, roll it into a ball, cover it with plastic wrap, and refrigerate; this will be the chick's head. Form the remaining mixture into an egg shape, cover it with plastic wrap, and refrigerate for at least 2 hours or overnight.

Before serving, roll the ball and egg shape in the remaining cheddar cheese until covered. Set the egg shape on its side on a platter, pressing it down a bit until it looks like a chick's body. Set the head on top of the body. Cut a raisin in half and stick into the cheese ball for the chick's eyes. Use the almond for the beak. Slice slivers from the carrot and use for the chick's feet.

Serve with crackers.

- 2½ cups shredded sharp orange cheddar cheese
- 6 ounces cream cheese, softened
- ¾ cup chopped drained pimientos
- 2 tablespoons finely chopped sweet white onion
- ¼ teaspoon smoked paprika
- ¼ teaspoon coarse salt
- Pinch cayenne pepper
- 1 dark raisin, 1 almond, and 1 carrot, for decorating

Crackers, for serving

pineapple-pineapple

serves 15 to 20

The pineapple is a symbol for hospitality and friendship and serves as an image of welcome . . . not unlike the appetizer. Nothing will welcome friends better than a pineapple-flavored, pineapple-shaped appetizer.

Cut the green tops off the scallions; set aside. From the white parts of the scallions, chop 1 tablespoon and reserve.

Using a stand mixer or a bowl and a spatula, mix together the cream cheese, cheddar, pineapple, jalapeño, cumin, salt, and the reserved tablespoon chopped scallions until combined. Form the mixture into a ball, cover with plastic wrap, and refrigerate for at least 2 hours or overnight.

Before serving, remove the cheese ball from the plastic, mold into a pineapple shape, and set it on a platter—it should look like an oval with a flat top. Arrange the pecans to look like the skin of a pineapple (you may need less than 2 cups, but choose the best-looking pecans to decorate the cheese ball). Stick the reserved green scallion tops in the top of the cheese ball to look like the crown of a pineapple.

Serve with crackers.

- 2 bunches scallions
- 16 ounces cream cheese, softened
- 1 cup shredded sharp white cheddar cheese
- One 8-ounce can crushed pineapple, drained well
- 1 small jalapeño, cored, seeded, and diced
- ½ teaspoon ground cumin
- ½ teaspoon coarse salt
- 2 cups pecan halves, toasted (see page 94), for decorating

Crackers, for serving

pizza-pizza

Just like with regular pizza, you can add whatever toppings you like best.

- 16 ounces cream cheese, softened

- 2½ cups shredded part-skim mozzarella cheese

- ¾ cup freshly grated Parmesan cheese

- ½ cup finely chopped pepperoni

- ¼ cup crushed tomatoes

- 2½ tablespoons chopped bell pepper, any color

- 1 tablespoon finely chopped onion

- 2 garlic cloves, minced or pressed through a garlic press

- ¾ teaspoon Italian seasoning

- ½ cup whole wheat breadcrumbs, for decorating

- Pepperoni slices and sliced pitted black olives (optional), for decorating

  Crackers or baguette slices, for serving

Using a stand mixer or a bowl and a spatula, mix together the cream cheese, 2 cups of the mozzarella (reserve ½ cup for decorating), Parmesan, chopped pepperoni, tomatoes 2 tablespoons of the bell pepper (reserve the ½ tablespoon for decorating), onion, garlic, and Italian seasoning. Form the mixture into a ball and loosely cover with plastic wrap. Gently flatten the ball into a disk; refrigerate for at least 2 hours or overnight.

Before serving, unwrap the disk and roll the edges in the breadcrumbs, pressing the middle in a bit as you roll. Set the disk on a plate and top with the remaining ½ cup of mozzarella, pepperoni slices, the remaining ½ tablespoon bell pepper, and olives, if using.

Serve with crackers or baguette slices.

port wine cheese ball

Wine cheese has been a party staple at family gatherings as far back as I can remember, but it took me twenty years to realize that the hunk of ruby red and fluorescent orange cheese coated in soggy pecans, surrounded by Triscuits, was not a product with ties to nature. Leave the wine cheese at the store—it's so processed that it'll be there, sitting on its Styrofoam tray, months later if you decide you still need it—and make your own wine cheese instead. I prefer white cheddar cheese; if you use orange cheese with the port, the resulting mixture will be a brownish color.

Using a stand mixer or a bowl and a spatula, mix together the cream cheese, cheddar, wine, and salt. Form the mixture into a ball, cover with plastic wrap, and refrigerate for at least 2 hours or overnight.

Before serving, roll the ball in the pecans to coat.

Serve with baguette slices or crackers.

- 8 ounces cream cheese, softened

- 2 cups shredded mild white cheddar cheese

- ½ cup port wine

- ½ teaspoon coarse salt

- 1 cup chopped pecans, toasted (see page 94), for coating

Baguette slices or crackers, for serving

the S.O.S.

When I was a kid, my dad used to regale us with stories about sh*t on a shingle, a dish he was served when he was in the Marines that consisted of chipped beef in cream sauce (aka sh*t), served over toast (the shingle). It was my favorite story of his because of the bad words. When researching cheese ball recipes, I found that chipped beef is a popular cheese ball add-in, so I developed this recipe in remembrance of my youth. This sh*t's for you, Dad.

serves
12 to 15

- 16 ounces cream cheese, softened
- 1 cup shredded sharp cheddar cheese
- ½ cup chopped chipped dried beef
- 1 teaspoon Dijon mustard
- 1 teaspoon Worcestershire sauce
- Dash hot sauce, such as Frank's RedHot
- 1 bunch scallions, chopped, for coating

Melba toast, for serving

Using a stand mixer or a bowl and a spatula, mix together the cream cheese, cheddar, beef, mustard, Worcestershire sauce, and hot sauce until combined. Form the mixture into a ball, cover with plastic wrap, and refrigerate for at least 2 hours or overnight.

Before serving, roll the cheese ball in the scallions to coat.

Serve with Melba toast.

spicy corn ball

serves
12 to 15

I made this once for a Cinco de Mayo fiesta, and a family member, whose name I will not mention, ate nearly the entire thing. It's that good. I recommend issuing a warning to guests: Save room for tacos.

Using a stand mixer or a bowl and a spatula, mix together the cream cheese, cheddar, corn, scallions, chipotle, 2 tablespoons of the chopped cilantro (reserve the rest for coating the cheese ball), garlic, cumin, and salt until combined. Form the mixture into a ball and cover with plastic wrap; refrigerate for at least 2 hours or overnight.

Before serving, roll in the remaining cilantro to coat.

Serve with crackers.

- 8 ounces cream cheese, softened
- 1 cup shredded sharp cheddar cheese
- 1 cup corn, canned or frozen, thawed and drained well
- 1/4 cup chopped scallions
- 2 tablespoons chopped canned chipotle in adobo
- 3/4 cup chopped fresh cilantro
- 1 garlic clove, chopped
- 1 1/2 tablespoons ground cumin
- 1/4 teaspoon coarse salt

Corn chips or crackers, for serving

spider

You should be able to find purple bell peppers in most grocery stores, but if you can't, use green bell peppers for the spider's legs.

- 16 ounces cream cheese, softened

- 1 cup shredded sharp white cheddar cheese

- 1/2 cup chopped pitted green olives

- 1 small garlic clove, chopped

- 1/2 cup poppy seeds, for coating

- 1 green or purple bell pepper, 1 pitted green olive, and 6 to 8 slivered almonds, for decorating

Crackers and celery sticks, for serving

Using a stand mixer or a bowl and a spatula, mix together the cream cheese, cheddar, chopped olives, and garlic. Form the mixture into a ball, cover with plastic wrap, and refrigerate for at least 2 hours or overnight.

Before serving, roll the cheese ball in the poppy seeds. Slice the pepper crosswise to make 8 slices, remove seeds, and slice into each round once. Arrange 4 pepper slices on each side of the spider for the legs. Slice the olive lengthwise for the eyes, and arrange the almonds for the teeth.

Serve with crackers and celery sticks.

tip To evenly coat the ball in poppy seeds, pour the seeds into a cereal bowl and set the cheese ball on top. Roll the bowl around the counter in a circular motion until the bottom half of the ball is evenly coated. Flip the ball over and roll around until the entire ball is coated.

the pigskin

Pig out: This football is thrice infused with bacon—the jalapeño is cooked in bacon grease, there's bacon mixed into the cheese, and bacon covers the football.

- 1½ pounds sliced bacon

- 1 medium jalapeño, cored, seeded, and finely chopped (if you want extra heat in your cheese ball, retain some of the seeds)

- 16 ounces cream cheese, softened

- 1 cup shredded sharp white cheddar cheese, plus 1 tablespoon, for decorating

- 1 tablespoon chopped scallions

Crackers, for serving

COOK THE BACON: Preheat the oven to 400°F. Lay the bacon slices in a single layer on 2 baking sheets. Bake until crispy, 15 to 20 minutes. Drain the bacon on paper towels and let cool. Reserve 2 tablespoons of the bacon grease from the pans, and discard the rest. Once the bacon has cooled, coarsely chop and set aside.

Cook the jalapeño in the reserved bacon grease in a small skillet over medium heat until soft, about 5 minutes. Using a stand mixer or a bowl and a spatula, mix together 1 cup of the chopped bacon, the sautéed jalapeño, cream cheese, 1 cup of the cheddar, and the scallions until combined. Form the mixture into a ball and cover with plastic wrap; refrigerate for at least 2 hours or overnight.

Before serving, form the ball into an oblong football shape and roll in the remaining chopped bacon to coat. Decorate the top of the football cheese ball with the remaining 1 tablespoon cheddar to resemble laces.

Serve with crackers.

the spaniard

Chorizo is a Spanish sausage and Manchego a mild Spanish cheese with a nutty flavor; both are readily available in most grocery stores or in specialty stores. If you haven't cooked with smoked paprika before, don't leave it out of this recipe. Once you've used it for this Spanish-style cheese ball, sprinkle it on eggs, roasted potatoes, or vegetables.

Using a stand mixer or a bowl and a spatula, mix together the cream cheese, Manchego, chorizo, roasted peppers, paprika, and scallions until combined. Form the mixture into a ball, cover with plastic wrap, and refrigerate for at least 2 hours or overnight.

Before serving, roll the cheese ball in the almonds to coat.

Serve with crackers or baguette slices.

- 8 ounces cream cheese, softened

- 2 cups shredded Manchego cheese

- ½ cup chopped chorizo (casing removed first)

- 2 tablespoons chopped roasted red peppers, patted dry

- ⅛ teaspoon smoked paprika

- 2 teaspoons chopped scallions

- 1 cup chopped unsalted almonds, preferably Marcona, toasted (see page 94), for coating

Crackers or baguette slices, for serving

herbed turkey

This turkey won't overshadow the main one if you serve him on Thanksgiving—it is Turkey Day, after all.

- 8 ounces cream cheese, softened

- 6 ounces goat cheese, softened

- 1 ½ tablespoons herbes de Provence

- 1 garlic clove, minced

- 1 teaspoon Dijon mustard

- Coarse salt, to taste

- ¾ cup slivered almonds, toasted (see page 94) and chopped, for coating

- 1 dark raisin, 1 whole almond, small piece red bell pepper, dried papaya or orange bell pepper slices, and thin pretzel sticks, for decorating

Crackers and crudités, for serving

Using a stand mixer or a bowl and a spatula, mix together the cream cheese, goat cheese, herbes de Provence, garlic, mustard, and salt. Form the mixture into a ball, cover with plastic wrap, and refrigerate for 2 hours or overnight.

Before serving, pinch a walnut-sized portion of the cheese mixture from the ball; you will use that for the turkey's head. Re-form the remaining cheese into a ball and roll the ball in the almonds. Roll the remaining portion of cheese into a small ball and set it on top of the larger ball—this is the turkey's head. Cut the raisin in half and place each half on the head for the eyes. Place the almond in the middle for the beak, and arrange the small piece of red pepper under the beak for the turkey's wattle. Stick dried papaya or orange bell pepper slices into the bottom of the cheese ball for the feet. Last, arrange pretzel sticks on the back of the cheese ball to look like tail feathers.

Serve with crackers and crudités.

veggie cream cheese bagel ball

serves
12 to 15

Like the Lox Bagel Ball on page 46, this cheese ball can take the place of the tub of cream cheese you usually set out at brunch, or it can be served beyond the a.m. with bagel chips or sliced vegetables.

Place ¼ cup carrots (reserve the remaining carrots for coating the cheese ball) and the bell pepper in a clean kitchen towel or sturdy paper towels and gather at the top. Squeeze the carrots and pepper to remove as much moisture as possible.

Using a stand mixer or a bowl and a spatula, mix together the carrots, bell pepper, cream cheese, radishes, 2 tablespoons scallions (reserve the remaining scallions for coating the cheese ball), jalapeño, if using, and salt until combined. Form the mixture into a ball, cover with plastic wrap, and refrigerate for at least 2 hours or overnight.

Before serving, roll the cheese ball in the remaining carrots and scallions to coat.

Serve with bagels, bagel chips, or crudités.

- ¾ cup shredded carrots
- ¼ cup chopped red bell pepper
- 16 ounces cream cheese, softened
- ¼ cup chopped radishes
- ½ cup chopped scallions
- 1 teaspoon chopped jalapeño (optional)
- ½ teaspoon coarse salt

Bagels, bagel chips, or crudités, for serving

white wine & gorgonzola log

While not technically a ball, the cheese log is the cheese ball's very close cousin. Or maybe closer, like a half-sister. Most cheese balls can be formed into logs and vice versa, but cheese mixtures with a lot of liquid, like wine, will hold their shape best when formed into a log rather than a ball.

Using a stand mixer or a bowl and a spatula, mix together the cream cheese, Gorgonzola, Chardonnay, shallots, salt, and pepper until combined. Form the mixture into a log, cover with plastic wrap, and refrigerate for at least 2 hours or overnight.

When ready to serve, roll the log in the pecans to coat.

Serve with crackers or toasted baguette slices.

- 16 ounces cream cheese, softened
- 3 ounces Gorgonzola cheese
- ½ cup Chardonnay
- 1 tablespoon finely chopped shallots
- Coarse salt, to taste
- Ground white pepper, to taste
- 1 cup chopped pecans, toasted (see page 94), for coating

Crackers or toasted baguette slices, for serving

5-MINUTE APPETIZER: CHEESE LOG

A cheese ball is the world's easiest appetizer, but if you're pressed for time, you may not have the extra 2 hours of chilling time required to make one. Good news: You can still make a fancy appetizer in a few seconds by dressing up a store-bought goat cheese log. Just unwrap the log and roll it in any of these combinations and serve with assorted crackers. Then sit back, relax, and wait for the compliments.

toasted pistachios + dried cranberries

toasted smoked almonds + chopped dried apricots; drizzle with honey before serving

toasted pine nuts + chopped fresh basil + grated lemon zest

chopped sun-dried tomatoes + minced garlic + chopped fresh thyme

chopped dried figs + chopped prosciutto + chopped fresh basil

beer-pretzel ball

You'll need just a cup of beer for this cheese ball, but buy a six-pack or a case; it's not redundant to eat this pretzel-covered beer-spiked snack with a frosty mug of beer.

Using a stand mixer or a bowl and a spatula, mix together the Swiss, cheddar, cream cheese, shallots, beer, Worcestershire sauce, salt, and hot sauce. Form the mixture into a ball and cover with plastic wrap. Refrigerate for at least 2 hours or overnight.

Before serving, roll the cheese ball in the pretzels to coat.

Serve with crackers or thick pretzels.

- 4 cups shredded Swiss cheese
- 5 cups shredded sharp white cheddar cheese
- 5 ounces cream cheese, softened
- 2 tablespoons chopped shallots
- 1 cup ale, such as Bass
- ½ teaspoon Worcestershire sauce
- ¼ teaspoon coarse salt
- Dash hot sauce, such as Frank's RedHot
- 4 ounces pretzels, crushed, for coating

Crackers or thick pretzels, for serving

date & blue cheese pops

Some of the best treats are on sticks—kebabs, lollipops, and Popsicles—but the way to one-up a snack on a stick? Make the stick edible.

makes
about
25 pops

- 8 ounces cream cheese, softened

- 3 ounces soft blue cheese

- 4 to 6 dates, pitted and chopped (about ½ cup)

- Pinch cayenne pepper (optional)

- 2 cups chopped pecans, toasted (see page 94), for coating

- 25 pretzel sticks

Using a stand mixer or a bowl and a spatula, mix together the cream cheese, blue cheese, dates, and cayenne, if using. Roll into 1-inch balls, cover with plastic wrap, and refrigerate for at least 2 hours or overnight.

Before serving, roll the balls in the pecans to coat, and insert a pretzel stick into each.

pesto holiday wreath

If you chop the basil used for decorating the top of the wreath it will bruise and turn black, so snip it into bits using kitchen shears instead and it will stay nice and green.

serves
12 to 15

- 16 ounces cream cheese, softened
- ³/₄ cup pesto (to make your own, see below)
- 6 to 10 snipped fresh basil leaves, for decorating
- 2 to 4 sun-dried tomatoes (not in oil), cut into pieces, for decorating
- Baguette slices, for serving

Using a stand mixer or a bowl and a spatula, mix together the cream cheese and pesto. Drop spoonfuls of the mixture onto a platter in a circular pattern with the edges touching each other. Smooth the spoonfuls together to form a wreath shape. Cover with plastic wrap and refrigerate for at least 2 hours or overnight.

Before serving, sprinkle the basil over the top of the wreath and decorate with pieces of sun-dried tomato.

Serve with baguette slices.

pesto

makes 1 cup

- 2 cups packed fresh basil leaves
- ¹/₂ cup extra-virgin olive oil
- ¹/₂ cup freshly grated Parmesan cheese
- ¹/₄ cup pine nuts
- 2 garlic cloves
- Coarse salt and freshly ground black pepper, to taste

Combine the basil, oil, Parmesan, pine nuts, garlic, and salt and pepper in a food processor and pulse until coarsely chopped. Season with additional salt and pepper if needed.

tip Use leftover pesto on pasta or spread on a sandwich, or freeze for up to 3 months.

white cheddar–horseradish baseball

serves 8 to 10

Baseball and cheese, two American icons meant to be together.

Using a stand mixer or a bowl and a spatula, mix together the cheddar, cream cheese, horseradish, lemon juice, Worcestershire sauce, and salt. Form the mixture into a ball, cover with plastic wrap, and refrigerate for at least 2 hours or overnight.

Slice the bell pepper into thin strips, then cut into pieces to look like baseball laces. Pat the pepper pieces dry with a paper towel. When ready to serve, put the ball on a platter and arrange the red pepper pieces to look like laces.

Serve with crackers.

- 2 cups shredded extra-sharp white cheddar cheese
- 4 ounces cream cheese, softened
- 3 tablespoons prepared horseradish
- ½ teaspoon fresh lemon juice
- Dash Worcestershire sauce
- Coarse salt, to taste
- 1 red bell pepper, for decorating

Crackers, for serving

french onion pyramid

This cheese mixture isn't smooth like other cheese balls; instead it's chunky from the onions and shredded Gruyère. It works best when molded—I found a pyramid-shaped mold at the kitchen supply store and love the way the golden cheese spread looks when molded in that, but you can use a loaf pan, too.

special
equipment:
pyramid-shaped
mold

serves
12 to 15

- 2 tablespoons unsalted butter

- 4 sweet onions, such as Vidalia, thinly sliced

- 1 teaspoon coarse salt

- 1½ cups dry white wine

- 2 cups shredded Gruyère cheese

- 6 ounces cream cheese, softened

- Pinch cayenne pepper

Crackers or toasted baguette slices, for serving

Line the mold (or a mini loaf pan) with plastic wrap, leaving an overhang on all sides.

Melt the butter in a skillet over medium heat. Once melted, add a quarter of the onion slices and sprinkle with some of the salt. Repeat layers of onions and salt until you've added all the onions to the skillet. Cook the onions without stirring for about 20 minutes. After that, stir the onions occasionally until they turn golden brown and are reduced in volume, 45 minutes to 1 hour. (Don't worry if any of the onions get a little burned.) Add the wine and cook until the wine reduces and the onions become syrupy. Remove the onions from the heat and cool completely, about 30 minutes.

Using a stand mixer or a bowl and a spatula, mix together the onion mixture, Gruyère, cream cheese, and cayenne until combined. Pack the mixture into the prepared mold, cover with plastic wrap, and refrigerate for at least 2 hours.

Before serving, remove from the mold and remove the plastic wrap.

Serve with crackers or toasted baguette slices.

sweet recipes

boozy cherry log

Like cherries jubilee without the fire, and in cheese form. This one's sweet like a cheesecake, but not too, so it could be served as either a dessert or an appetizer. If you're serving it as a starter, put out water crackers, but for dessert, serve it with graham crackers.

Stir together the cherries, rum, and sugar and let sit for 1 hour, stirring occasionally, until the sugar dissolves.

Using a stand mixer or a bowl and a spatula, mix together the cherry mixture, cream cheese, and vanilla until combined. Form the mixture into a log, cover with plastic wrap, and refrigerate for at least 2 hours or overnight.

Before serving, roll the log in the pecans to coat.

Serve with water crackers or graham crackers.

- 1 cup chopped dried Bing cherries
- ½ cup light rum
- 1 cup sugar
- 16 ounces cream cheese, softened
- 1 teaspoon pure vanilla extract
- 1 cup chopped pecans, toasted (see page 94), for coating

Water crackers or graham crackers, for serving

bald eagles

Ever notice how cashews look exactly like the beaks on birds of prey? I did. When you make these little birds, dip in the coconut first and hold on to that part when you dip the cheese ball into the chocolate cookies; if you do the opposite, you'll get chocolate-cookie fingerprints on your eagles' heads.

makes about 15 eagles

- 16 ounces cream cheese, softened

- ½ cup confectioners' sugar

- 1 teaspoon pure vanilla extract

- 1 cup unsweetened coconut flakes, for decorating

- 8 to 10 chocolate wafer cookies, finely crushed, for decorating

- 15 whole cashews, for decorating

- Mini chocolate chips or sliced dark raisins, for decorating

Using a stand mixer or a bowl and a spatula, mix together the cream cheese, sugar, and vanilla extract until combined. Form into 15 small, egg-shaped balls, about 2 tablespoons each, and set on a baking sheet. Cover with plastic wrap and refrigerate the cheese balls for at least 2 hours or overnight.

Before serving, dip the top of each ball into the coconut. Holding on to the coconut-coated portion, dip the bottom portion into the cookies; set each cheese ball down, coconut side up. Stick a cashew into each as a beak and use mini chocolate chips or sliced raisins for the eyes.

inside-out carrot cake

serves
15 to 20

Everyone loves carrot cake, but if you ask me, it's just a vehicle for the cream cheese frosting. This not-too-sweet cheese ball is what carrot cake should be: a few carrots and a whole lot of cream cheese frosting.

Place the carrots in a clean kitchen towel or sturdy paper towels and gather at the top. Squeeze the carrots to remove as much moisture as possible.

Using a stand mixer or a bowl and a spatula, mix together the carrots, cream cheese, raisins, pineapple, sugar, orange juice, and vanilla extract until combined. Form the mixture into a ball and cover with plastic wrap; refrigerate for at least 2 hours or overnight.

Before serving, roll the ball in the walnuts to coat.

Serve with vanilla wafer cookies, graham crackers, or carrot sticks.

- 2 cups shredded carrots
- 16 ounces cream cheese, softened
- $\frac{1}{4}$ cup dark raisins
- $\frac{1}{4}$ cup crushed pineapple, drained well
- $\frac{1}{4}$ cup confectioners' sugar
- 1 tablespoon orange juice
- 1 teaspoon pure vanilla extract
- 1 cup walnuts, toasted (see Tip), for coating

Vanilla wafer cookies, graham crackers, or carrot sticks, for serving

tip TO TOAST NUTS: Preheat oven to 350°F. Arrange nuts on a baking sheet in a single layer. Bake for 8 to 10 minutes, checking frequently, until golden brown and fragrant.

chocolate–peanut butter reindeer

serves
15 to 20

This is one of those indulgent desserts where people take one bite and say, "It's so rich, I can't eat another bite," then eat, like, six more bites. The chocolate–peanut butter combination is pretty rich, but the nature of a cheese ball is that you can serve yourself little bites without overdoing it.

- 2 cups semisweet chocolate chips

- 8 ounces cream cheese, softened

- 3/4 cup creamy peanut butter

- 1/2 cup confectioners' sugar

- 1 teaspoon pure vanilla extract

- 2 pretzels; 2 chocolate candies, such as M&M's or Reese's Pieces; and 1 red gumdrop, for decorating

Chocolate cookies, pretzels, or vanilla wafer cookies, for serving

In a double boiler or a glass bowl set over simmering water, melt the chocolate. Let cool for 15 minutes.

Using a stand mixer or a bowl and a spatula, blend the cream cheese, melted chocolate, peanut butter, sugar, and vanilla extract. Form the mixture into a ball, cover with plastic wrap, and refrigerate for at least 2 hours or overnight.

Before serving, set the ball on a platter. Break the pretzels into antler shapes and add to each side of the cheese ball. Use the chocolate candies for the eyes and the gumdrop for the nose.

Serve with chocolate cookies, pretzels, or vanilla wafers.

sweet almond hedgehog

serves
12 to 15

I've seen hedgehogs in pet stores near the hamsters and guinea pigs. I don't know if they make good companion animals, but I do know that their likeness makes an adorable cheese ball.

Crush 2 tablespoons of the almonds and set the remaining slivers aside.

Using a stand mixer or a bowl and a spatula, mix together the 2 tablespoons crushed almonds, the cream cheese, sugar, almond extract, and vanilla extract until combined. Form the mixture into a ball, cover with plastic wrap, and refrigerate for at least 2 hours or overnight.

Before serving, unwrap the cheese ball and form into the shape of a hedgehog, like a teardrop. Arrange the remaining almonds on the back of the hedgehog to look like quills (choose the ones with the best shape for the quills). Cut 1 raisin in half for each of the eyes and put a whole raisin at the tip of the hedgehog's face for the nose.

Serve with vanilla wafer cookies.

- 1 cup slivered almonds, toasted (see page 94)
- 16 ounces cream cheese, softened
- ½ cup confectioners' sugar
- 1 teaspoon pure almond extract
- ½ teaspoon pure vanilla extract
- 2 dark raisins, for decorating

Vanilla wafer cookies, for serving

lemon-ginger cheesecake truffles

Stack bite-sized lemon cheesecake bites like a tower of snowballs ready for a snowball fight, or in this case, a lemon cheesecake truffle–eating contest.

- 16 ounces cream cheese, softened
- 1 cup confectioners' sugar
- Zest of 2 lemons, grated
- 1½ teaspoons chopped candied ginger (optional)
- 1 teaspoon fresh lemon juice
- ½ teaspoon pure vanilla extract
- 1 cup crushed gingersnaps, for coating

Using a stand mixer or a bowl and a spatula, mix together the cream cheese, sugar, lemon zest, candied ginger, if using, lemon juice, and vanilla extract. Roll into twenty 1-inch balls, cover with plastic wrap, and refrigerate for at least 2 hours or overnight.

Before serving, roll each ball in the gingersnaps to coat.

tip Zest the lemons over your mixing bowl; when they're zested, the lemon oil is released, which will add more lemon flavor to your recipe.

new york–style cheesecake spread

This super-easy dessert is like a spreadable, no-bake version of cheesecake.

Using a stand mixer or a bowl and a spatula, mix together the cream cheese, sugar, sour cream, lemon zest, and vanilla extract until combined. Form the mixture into a ball and cover loosely with plastic wrap. Gently flatten the ball into a disk; refrigerate for at least 2 hours or overnight.

Before serving, unwrap the disk and roll the edges in the crushed graham crackers, pressing the middle in a bit as you roll. Set the disk on a plate and top with the sliced strawberries.

Serve with graham crackers and whole strawberries.

- 16 ounces cream cheese, softened
- ½ cup confectioners' sugar
- 1 tablespoon sour cream
- 1 teaspoon grated lemon zest
- 1 teaspoon pure vanilla extract
- 3 graham crackers, crushed, for coating
- Sliced strawberries, for decorating

Graham crackers and whole strawberries, for serving

orange creamsicle cheese ball

One retro treat meets another: a cheese ball that tastes just like the classic ice cream bar.

- 16 ounces cream cheese, softened

- ½ cup confectioners' sugar

- 3 tablespoons frozen orange juice concentrate, unthawed

- 1 tablespoon orange marmalade

- 2 teaspoons pure vanilla extract

- 8 graham crackers, crushed, for coating

Graham crackers, vanilla wafer cookies, or fruit, for serving

Using a stand mixer or a bowl and a spatula, mix together the cream cheese, sugar, orange juice concentrate, marmalade, and vanilla extract. Form the mixture into a ball and cover with plastic wrap; refrigerate for at least 2 hours or overnight.

Before serving, roll the cheese ball in the crushed graham crackers to coat.

Serve with graham crackers, vanilla wafer cookies, or fruit.

s'mores ball

Campfire-inspired, but no kindling needed.

- 8 ounces semisweet chocolate
- ½ cup packed light brown sugar
- 8 ounces cream cheese, softened
- 1 teaspoon pure vanilla extract
- 1 cup mini marshmallows
- 8 graham crackers, crushed, for coating

Graham crackers, for serving

In a double boiler or a glass bowl set over a pot of simmering water, melt the chocolate. When smooth, remove from the water and add the sugar. Stir until combined and let cool, about 15 minutes.

Using a stand mixer or a bowl and a spatula, mix together the chocolate mixture, cream cheese, and vanilla extract until combined and even colored. Blend in the marshmallows. Form the mixture into a ball, cover with plastic wrap, and refrigerate for at least 2 hours or overnight.

Before serving, roll the cheese ball in the crushed graham crackers to coat.

Serve with graham crackers.

triple-chocolate ball

serves 15 to 20

Adding espresso powder to chocolate makes it richer (but not coffee-flavored), but if you leave it out, this dessert will still be chocolaty and decadent.

In a double boiler or a glass bowl set over simmering water, melt the semisweet chocolate and unsweetened chocolate, stirring occasionally. When smooth, remove from the water and add the sugar. Stir until combined and let cool, about 15 minutes.

Using a stand mixer or a bowl and a spatula, blend the chocolate mixture, cream cheese, cocoa powder, vanilla extract, and espresso powder, if using. Form the mixture into a ball, cover with plastic wrap, and refrigerate for at least 2 hours or overnight.

Before serving, roll the cheese ball in the chocolate chips to coat.

Serve with chocolate cookies or vanilla wafer cookies.

- 8 ounces semisweet chocolate
- 2 ounces unsweetened chocolate
- $\frac{1}{2}$ cup sugar
- 16 ounces cream cheese, softened
- $\frac{1}{4}$ cup unsweetened cocoa powder
- 1 teaspoon pure vanilla extract
- 1 teaspoon espresso powder (optional)
- 1 cup mixed chocolate and white chocolate chips, for coating

Chocolate cookies or vanilla wafer cookies, for serving

oreo cheesecake truffles

You can crush the cookies in a bag with a rolling pin, but come on—haven't you always wanted to smash cookies with your bare hands?

- 16 ounces cream cheese, softened

- ¾ cup confectioners' sugar

- 1½ teaspoons pure vanilla extract

- 20 Oreo cookies, coarsely crushed by hand, plus 10 Oreo cookies, finely crushed, for coating

Using a stand mixer or a bowl and a spatula, mix together the cream cheese, sugar, vanilla extract, and the coarsely crushed Oreo cookies. Roll the mixture into twenty-four 1-inch balls, cover with plastic wrap, and refrigerate for at least 2 hours or overnight.

Before serving, roll each ball in the finely crushed Oreo crumbs to coat.

patriotic berry cheese ball

serves
12 to 15

Nature gave us red and blue berries fit for decorating all manner of patriotic treats, and a sweet ball of cheese is no exception.

Using a stand mixer or a bowl and a spatula, mix together the cream cheese, sugar, jam, and vanilla extract until combined. Form the mixture into a ball, cover with plastic wrap, and refrigerate for at least 2 hours or overnight.

Before serving, decorate the cheese ball with the berries.

Serve with graham crackers or vanilla wafer cookies.

- 16 ounces cream cheese, softened
- $\frac{1}{2}$ cup confectioners' sugar
- $\frac{1}{4}$ cup strawberry or raspberry jam
- 1 teaspoon pure vanilla extract
- $1\frac{1}{2}$ cups mixed fresh raspberries and blueberries, for decorating

Graham crackers or vanilla wafer cookies, for serving

peanut butter starfish

special
equipment:
starfish mold,
from a beach
toy set

serves
12 to 15

It was my intention to make a plain old peanut butter
cheese ball, but then I saw a starfish mold in a set of beach
toys at the drugstore and immediately pictured a beach-
themed party with Swedish fish swimming in punch and
shark fin cupcakes. You can use any shape of beach toy to
mold the cream cheese mixture, or you can form it into
a traditional cheese ball; coat it with peanuts, crushed
peanut butter sandwich cookies, or graham crackers.

- 12 ounces cream cheese,
  softened

- 1 cup creamy peanut butter

- ¼ cup packed light brown
  sugar

- 1 teaspoon pure vanilla
  extract

- 10 peanut butter sandwich
  cookies, crushed, for
  decorating

Graham crackers, vanilla wafer
cookies, or peanut butter
sandwich cookies, for serving

Line the starfish mold with plastic wrap, leaving an overhang
on all sides.

Using a stand mixer or a bowl and a spatula, mix together
the cream cheese, peanut butter, sugar, and vanilla extract
until combined. Pack the mixture into the prepared starfish
mold, cover with plastic wrap, and refrigerate for at least
2 hours or overnight.

When ready to serve, spread the crushed peanut butter
sandwich cookies on a platter, and unmold the starfish
cheese ball onto the cookies. Remove the plastic wrap.
Gently press and release the flat part of a butter knife all
over the top of the starfish to create texture.

Serve with graham crackers, vanilla wafer cookies, or peanut
butter sandwich cookies.

special equipment: three or four 4-inch heart-shaped pans

serves 12 to 15

pink velvet hearts

It takes a lot of food coloring to turn cream cheese red; that's why these are pink velvet instead of red velvet. If you really want bright red, keep adding food coloring; just know that the resulting cheese balls may be a bit bitter.

Line heart-shaped pans with plastic wrap, leaving an overhang on all sides.

Using a stand mixer or a bowl and a spatula, mix together the cream cheese, sugar, cocoa powder, vanilla extract, and food coloring. Pack the mixture into the prepared pans. Cover with plastic wrap, and refrigerate for at least 2 hours or overnight.

Before serving, unmold the cheese mixture from the pans and set on a platter. Remove the plastic wrap. Using a vegetable peeler, shave white chocolate curls over the tops of the hearts, or top with white chocolate chips.

Serve with graham crackers or vanilla wafer cookies.

- 16 ounces cream cheese, softened
- 1 cup confectioners' sugar
- 2 tablespoons unsweetened cocoa powder
- 1 teaspoon pure vanilla extract
- 20 to 25 drops red food coloring
- White chocolate bar or white chocolate chips, for decorating

Graham crackers or vanilla wafer cookies, for serving

note This mixture can also be served as a traditional cheese ball. Instead of pressing the mixture into heart-shaped pans, form a ball, wrap in plastic wrap, and refrigerate for the same amount of time. Before serving, coat in semisweet or white chocolate chips.

coconut snowman

serves
12 to 15

You know how the song goes: "In the meadow we can build a coconut-covered cheese ball snowman. . . ."

Using a stand mixer or a bowl and a spatula, mix together the cream cheese, 1 cup of the coconut (reserve the remaining ½ cup for coating), the sugar, cream of coconut, and vanilla extract until combined. Roll the mixture into 3 balls in descending sizes. Cover the balls with plastic wrap and refrigerate for at least 2 hours or overnight.

Before serving, roll the balls in the remaining ½ cup coconut; set the largest ball on a platter and stack the 2 balls on top, using the smallest as the head. Decorate the face using the raisins for the eyes and mouth, the carrot sliver for the nose, the carrot strip as a scarf, pomegranate seeds for buttons, and the chocolate cookie as the snowman's hat.

Serve with graham crackers or chocolate or vanilla wafer cookies.

- 16 ounces cream cheese, softened

- 1½ cups unsweetened coconut flakes

- ½ cup confectioners' sugar

- 2 tablespoons cream of coconut (not coconut milk)

- 1½ teaspoons pure vanilla extract

- 3 dark raisins, 1 carrot sliver, 1 carrot strip, pomegranate seeds, and 1 chocolate cookie, for decorating

Graham crackers, chocolate cookies, or vanilla wafer cookies, for serving

witches' hats

Wickedly delicious two-bite desserts for your Halloween party buffet—they'll balance out the creepy treats like goblin-blood punch.

- 1 recipe mixture for Triple-Chocolate Ball (page 108) or Chocolate–Peanut Butter Reindeer (page 97)

- Chocolate cookies, for decorating

- White chocolate chips, for decorating

Prepare the mixture for either the Triple Chocolate Cheese Ball or the Chocolate–Peanut Butter Reindeer. Scoop out and roll into 1½-inch balls. Place on a tray, cover with plastic wrap, and refrigerate for at least 2 hours or overnight.

Before serving, pinch the top of each ball into a point, and set each triangle on top of a cookie. Set a chocolate chip in the center of each hat for the buckle.

special
equipment:
ramekins in
3 sizes: 1 ounce,
3 ounce, and
6 ounce

serves
8 to 10

wedding cake

A few years ago, bath towels rolled to look like wedding cakes were all the rage at bridal showers. Everyone's seen those about a million times, so wow your cousins and make your girlfriends jealous with a wedding cake cheese ball instead.

Line the 3 ramekins with plastic wrap, leaving an overhang.

Using a stand mixer or a bowl and a spatula, mix together the cream cheese, sugar, lemon zest, and vanilla extract. Pack the mixture into the prepared ramekins, leveling the top with a butter knife. Put the remaining cream cheese mixture in a plastic zip-top bag; refrigerate the ramekins and bag for at least 2 hours or overnight.

Before serving, overturn the largest ramekin onto a platter; remove the ramekin and the plastic wrap. The cheese will have wrinkles in it from the plastic wrap—to smooth the wrinkles, run a butter knife under hot water for 30 seconds and dry it with a towel. Use the warm knife to smooth out each layer of the cheese, repeating the water step when the knife cools. Gently overturn the 3-ounce ramekin onto the 6-ounce ramekin and the 1-ounce ramekin on top of that. To decorate the cake, snip the tip off a corner of the zip-top bag. Gently squeeze out beads of the cheese mixture along the bottom and top of each cake layer. (Or use a cake decorating bag and tips to decorate the cake.)

Serve with graham crackers and strawberries.

- 14 ounces cream cheese, softened
- ½ cup confectioners' sugar
- 1 teaspoon grated lemon zest
- 1 teaspoon pure vanilla extract

Graham crackers and strawberries, for serving

pumpkin-pumpkin

Pumpkin cheesecake is the kind of dessert you hope someone brings to Thanksgiving—it's richer than pumpkin pie and way more exciting, but it's kind of a pain to make. The answer to everyone's fall prayers: a no-bake pumpkin cheese ball that tastes just like pumpkin cheesecake and looks like a pumpkin.

serves
12 to 15

- 16 ounces cream cheese, softened
- ½ cup pumpkin puree (not pumpkin pie filling)
- ⅓ cup packed light brown sugar
- 1½ teaspoons ground cinnamon
- 1 teaspoon pure vanilla extract
- ½ teaspoon ground ginger
- ¼ teaspoon ground cloves
- Stem of a bell pepper and 1 sprig fresh cilantro, for decorating

Graham crackers or gingersnaps, for serving

Using a stand mixer or a bowl and a spatula, mix together the cream cheese, pumpkin, sugar, cinnamon, vanilla extract, ginger, and cloves until combined. Form the mixture into a ball and cover with plastic wrap; refrigerate for at least 2 hours or overnight.

Before serving, set the cheese ball on a platter and score it to resemble the lines on a pumpkin. Top with the pepper stem and wind the cilantro around the stem to look like the pumpkin's vines.

Serve with graham crackers or gingersnaps.

index

Page numbers in *italics* indicate illustrations.